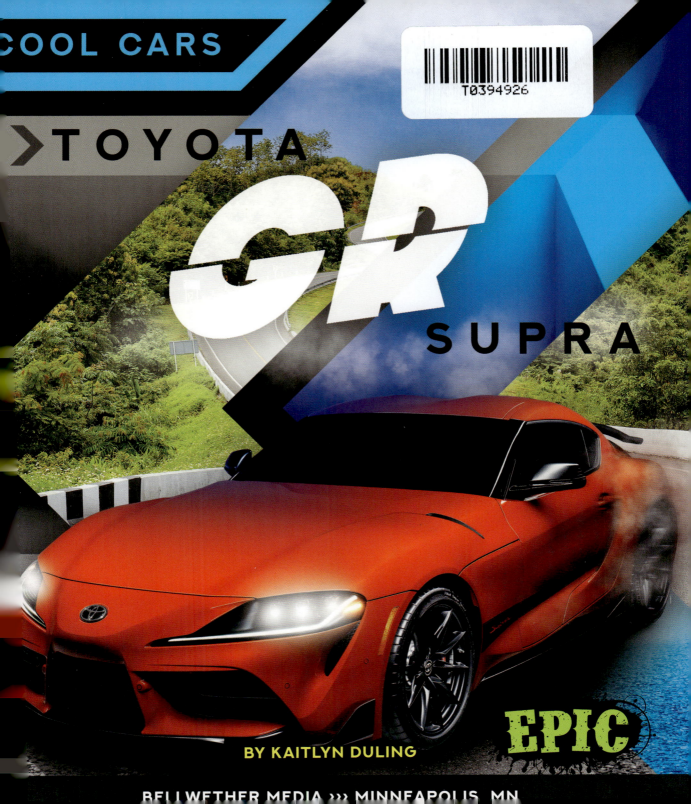
COOL CARS

TOYOTA GR SUPRA

BY KAITLYN DULING

BELLWETHER MEDIA ⟫⟫ MINNEAPOLIS, MN

EPIC

EPIC BOOKS are no ordinary books. They burst with intense action, high-speed heroics, and shadows of the unknown. Are you ready for an Epic adventure?

This edition first published in 2025 by Bellwether Media, Inc.

No part of this publication may be reproduced in whole or in part without written permission of the publisher. For information regarding permission, write to Bellwether Media, Inc., Attention: Permissions Department, 6012 Blue Circle Drive, Minnetonka, MN 55343.

Library of Congress Cataloging-in-Publication Data

LC record for Toyota GR Supra available at: https://lccn.loc.gov/2024039179

Text copyright © 2025 by Bellwether Media, Inc. EPIC and associcted logos are trademarks and/or registered trademarks of Bellwether Media, Inc.

Editor: Rachael Barnes   Designer: Gabriel Hilger

Printed in the United States of America, North Mankato, MN.

TABLE OF CONTENTS

SUPER SPORTY SUPRA	4
ALL ABOUT THE GR SUPRA	6
PARTS OF THE GR SUPRA	12
THE GR SUPRA'S FUTURE	20
GLOSSARY	22
TO LEARN MORE	23
INDEX	24

SUPER SPORTY SUPRA

A driver takes her Toyota GR Supra around a sharp corner. It easily grips the road.

The driver takes a turn onto the highway, quickly picking up speed. This sports car is a smooth ride!

ALL ABOUT THE GR SUPRA »

TOYOTA OFFICES IN JAPAN

KIICHIRO TOYODA

The Toyota Motor Corporation is based in Japan. Kiichiro Toyoda founded the company in the 1930s.

Today, Toyota is one of the world's top-selling car companies! The Corolla, Camry, and Prius are well-known **models**.

CAMRY

📍 WHERE WAS IT MADE?

AICHI, JAPAN

ASIA

SPORTS CAR FACTORY IN AUSTRIA

NAME GAME

GR stands for Gazoo Racing. *Supra* means "to go beyond." The name tells buyers the GR Supra can drive like a race car!

Toyota and BMW work together to build sports cars. They share a factory in Austria.

The GR Supra is built alongside the BMW Z4. The cars even share some of the same parts!

BMW Z4

The Toyota Supra was first sold in 1979. Several models were made. But Toyota stopped building Supra models in 2002.

In 2020, the Supra returned as the GR Supra! It is known for its smooth **handling**.

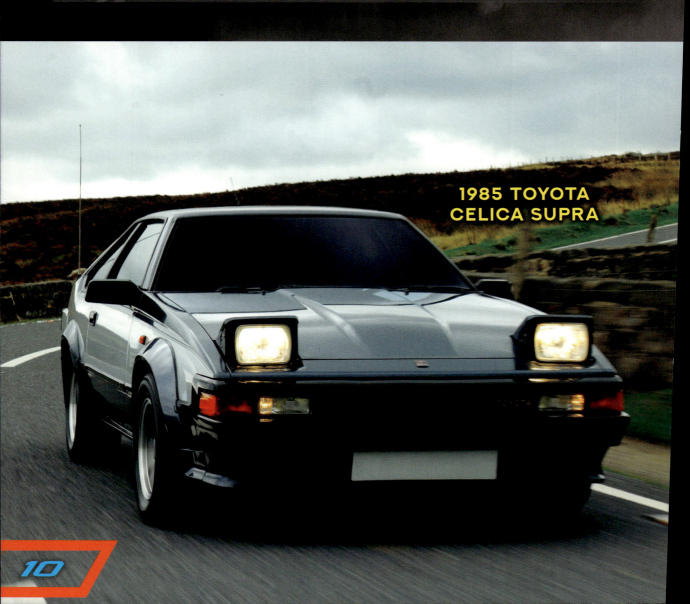

1985 TOYOTA CELICA SUPRA

10

GR SUPRA BASICS

YEAR FIRST MADE — 1979 as the Celica Supra

COST — starts at $56,250

HOW MANY MADE — currently in production

FEATURES

inline-six engine | fastback roofline | LED headlights

PARTS OF THE GR SUPRA

DOUBLE-BUBBLE FASTBACK ROOF

The GR Supra is a two-door **coupe**. It has a double-bubble **fastback** roof.

The car's bright **LED** headlights cut through the dark. Drivers can see the road at night.

LED HEADLIGHT

The GR Supra has a powerful **inline-six engine**. Its top speed is 155 miles (249 kilometers) per hour. The car can be built with a **manual transmission**. This gives drivers more control.

ENGINE SPECS

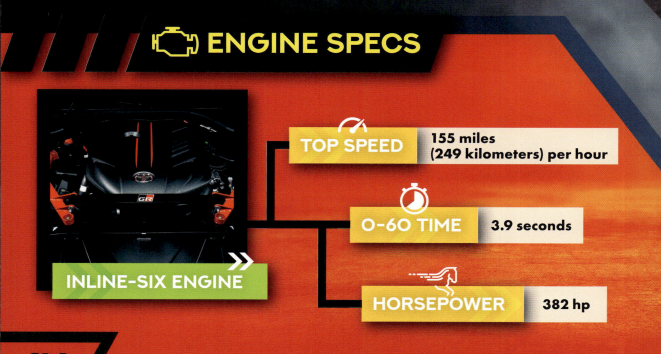

INLINE-SIX ENGINE

TOP SPEED — 155 miles (249 kilometers) per hour

0-60 TIME — 3.9 seconds

HORSEPOWER — 382 hp

The GR Supra has a large **grille**. There are also two large **air intakes** on the front of the car.

SIZE CHART

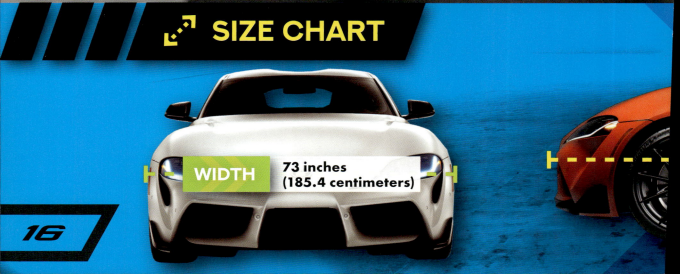

WIDTH — 73 inches (185.4 centimeters)

These parts let air flow past the engine. This keeps the engine cool.

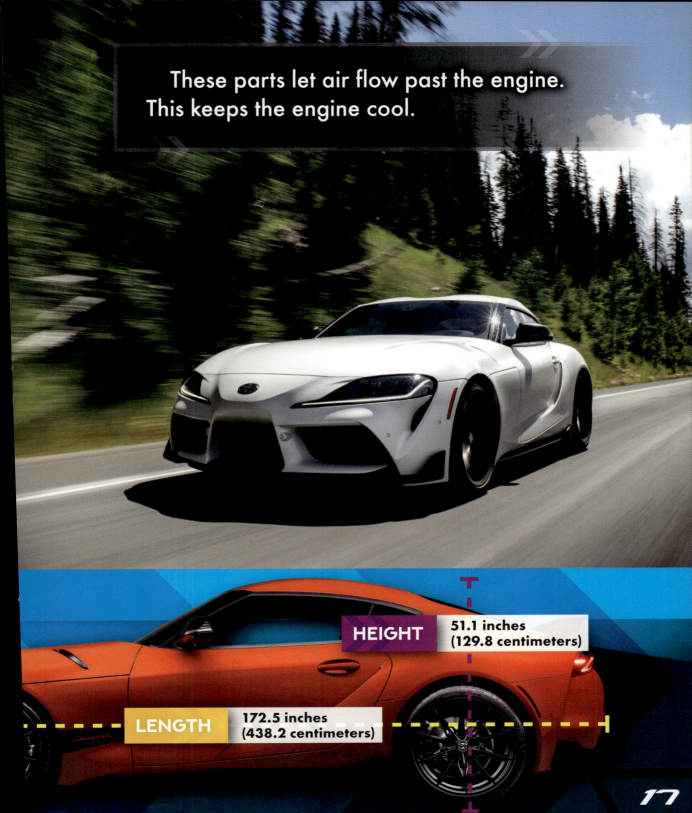

HEIGHT 51.1 inches (129.8 centimeters)

LENGTH 172.5 inches (438.2 centimeters)

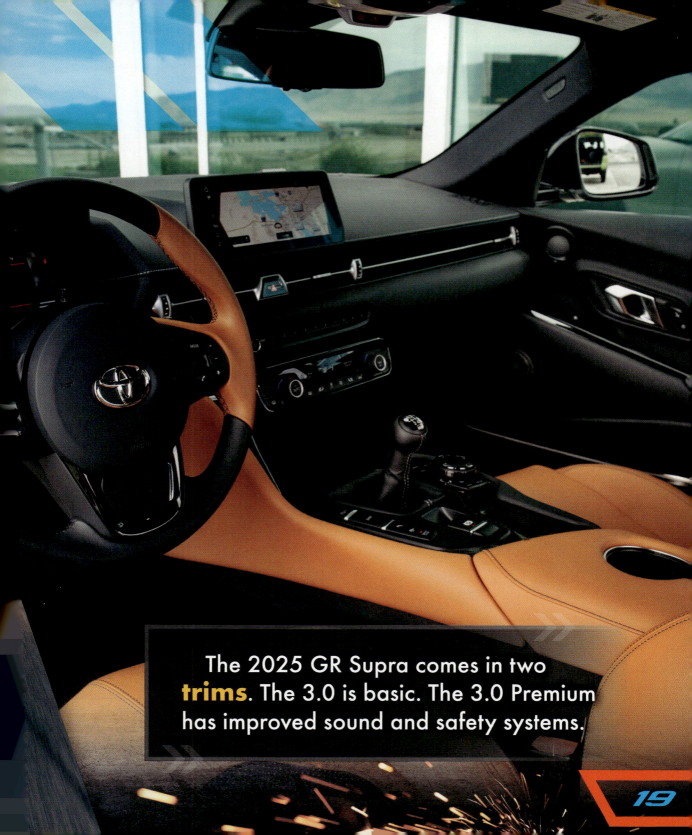

The 2025 GR Supra comes in two **trims**. The 3.0 is basic. The 3.0 Premium has improved sound and safety systems.

19

THE GR SUPRA'S FUTURE »

Toyota is releasing a more powerful model called the Supra GRMN. The GRMN has a racing model, too!

Toyota will keep working with other companies to build more sports cars. Fans cannot wait to see what they create!

FUEL OF THE FUTURE

Toyota is working on fuels that might someday replace gas. These "green fuels" could be better for Earth.

SUPRA GRMN RACING MODEL

GLOSSARY

air intakes—openings on a car that allow air to reach its engine

coupe—a car with a hard roof and two doors

fastback—related to a curved car roof with a long downward slope that reaches the rear bumper

grille—a set of bars that covers an opening on the front of a car; the grille allows air to enter and exit the engine.

handling—how a car performs around turns

inline-six engine—an engine with 6 cylinders arranged in a straight row

LED—related to lights that save energy and take a very long time to burn out

manual transmission—a system that a driver uses to shift gears

models—specific kinds of cars

spoiler—a part on the back of a car that helps the car grip the road

trims—models of a car with specific sets of features and equipment

TO LEARN MORE

AT THE LIBRARY

Duling, Kaitlyn. *Ferrari Roma*. Minneapolis, Minn.: Bellwether Media, 2025.

Respicio, Mae. *Sports Car Design*. North Mankato, Minn.: Capstone, 2025.

Webster, Christine. *BMW*. New York, N.Y.: AV2, 2022.

ON THE WEB

FACTSURFER

Factsurfer.com gives you a safe, fun way to find more information.

1. Go to www.factsurfer.com.

2. Enter "Toyota GR Supra" into the search box and click 🔍.

3. Select your book cover to see a list of related content.

INDEX

air intakes, 16, 17
Austria, 8
basics, 11
BMW, 8, 9
coupe, 12
engine, 14, 17
engine specs, 14
fuels, 21
grille, 16, 17
handling, 10
history, 6, 10
Japan, 6, 7
LED headlights, 13
manual transmission, 14
models, 7, 9, 10, 19, 20
name, 8

roof, 12
size, 16–17
speed, 5, 14
spoiler, 18
Supra GRMN, 20, 21
Toyoda, Kiichiro, 6
Toyota Motor Corporation, 6, 7, 8, 10, 20, 21
trims, 19

The images in this book are reproduced through the courtesy of: Toyota, front cover, pp. 4, 5, 7, 8, 11 (inline-six engine, fastback roofline, LED headlights), 13, 14, 15, 16 (air intake, grille, width), 17 (main, length), 18 (main, spoiler), 19, 20, 21; Artistic Operations, pp. 3, 12; Photo Japan/ Alamy, p. 6 (Toyota offices in Japan); unknown/ Wikipedia, p. 6 (Kiichiro Toyoda); BoJack, p. 9; Rob Scorah/ Alamy, p. 10; Roman Vasilenia, p. 11 (isolated GR Supra).